Frédéric Delalot

towards the party
At the end of the forest

KDP Editions

1

Time of the crowds...

Honey light, origin of coronations, pure trust

Transparent vials of a summer sky, millennials...

The pleasures were mooring...

All the parts of happiness, these unmissable turrets

Young years, innocuous victories...

We are of an expansionist opinion, often...

Then, I write a few lines, desire for freedom, season...

We were waiting for the end of the incessant noises, indefinite noise.

This arid hour must be invented...

Without the sea, since such curves do not last...

A thousand pages before us, through the intermittency of the heart

In how many worlds, facades...

Decidedly reflected the powerful hope

Canvases of the dawn, go to Peru, the Cordillera

Long necklaces, going up Sainte-Catherine...

Moments of grace, invincible journey...

Dreamlike, there was, there, an armada of projects...

Squarely on the edge...

Ah! in the distance, horses of light, splendid

Creative moments, coiled curtains, festive fatigue...

Formerly, appointment,

Whimsical rejoicing...

The August temperature consumed the virginity of the evening

Routes, panoramas...

Cities, sparkling slowness, ribambelles...

Energetic, immortal, our free, earthly figures

Some summer evenings, in the cellars...

Pinnacles of curves, so many times...

You were going to the foam, backwards...

From causes to consequences...

We were ourselves, ink...

They had clung to this dream, to this wandering ideal.

At the end of the world, attraction...

That we no longer thought to touch, ancient splendor

We were going through foggy, intoxicating parks

Towards mesmerizing horizons, almost purple.

2

Hotels and mezzanines, huge mirrors, Java bubbles...

Rebirths of psychic terroirs in eternal youth

Found, automatic revivals...

In a pile of sheets, there is this whole story

Then, I write a few lines, desire for freedom, season

We were waiting for the end of the incessant noises, indefinite din

And really, the time of the crowds

Ignoring routine, on the street...

Escapes from an illusion...

Leaves flew away in the nascent spring...

This is the means we had found, light, thought.

In Bastille or elsewhere, and still a few nights...

The same pattern was repeated continuously, with a regular interval

Moments of grace, invincible journey...

Dreamlike, there was, there, an armada of projects...

The light of this honey, origin of the coronations, pure confidence

Ah! in the distance, horses of light, splendid...

By the way, Hindu tunes

Crossovers

Memories of trips, expectation of the anchor

Quick street tours...

I was thinking about stealth happiness...

Everything seemed like a flyover, at first, an Island apart

Deep down, I liked straight lines, without too many people

On the travel trunk, there was a bouquet...

Who could have been hacienda, territory...

You were going to the foam, backwards, we were swimming a little

Transparent vials of a summer sky, millennials...

We were ourselves, ink...

Largesse, near the driveway

New times...

So, between two bays...

Illuminated ancestry of indirect projectors

Oasis

The Megalithic Night

Proclaim this nagging

Symphony.

3

The large park was gradually overflowing into the city

In the streets of the neighborhood, oil on canvas, broad strokes

Unbeatable happiness and joys, there were worlds

Each time, the bytes propelled us

Through how many enjoyable passages...

Playable, my body got drunk in my place

The pleasures were mooring

Nothing happens, everything remembers

Of a silence, wild animals, in the corners ...

In the past, there were bright orange nights

Horses stood out from the landscape and dreams

Happy transposition, and later, through vegetable gardens

There would be a multitude of garden dwarfs, shows

I wanted to describe, to whisper...

As under the sky of the rue des Taillandiers, emergence

All the parts of happiness, these unmissable turrets...

As long as the party does not return, with the gold of mirages ...

The large park was gradually overflowing into the city

Hotels and mezzanines, mirrors, Java bubbles...

The blank page was waiting for me, it was rushing...

Many fall asleep, life stretches...

Facades, perfect harmonies, here is the time

We saw them following an asteroid, trajectory

Changing, it was a meditative time

Moments lasted like pleasure

And the city, in the distance, was still waiting for us

Almost wild, preamble of the dawns...

Young years, innocuous victories...

Ephemeral, unexpected trips, blank pages

Even the world of tomorrow

Looks a bit like the material

Vital momentum, after that moment

Initiating relaxation, blue plants

Infinite touch

Myriad

Legendary

Heady.

4

It was another era, a century of experiences

Snow was announced, painted brick facades

Little red lanterns, I saw worlds

Escapades, and independences, perhaps...

Maybe it's a beginning, a presentation of the world...

At the borders, universal limit, what we can know

We are of an expansionist opinion, often...

Until we meet, the word is strong, our psyches...

The story we continued, the Avenue du Levant...

We listened to Radio Vitamine, before going out again

In Paris, there was an inner courtyard, a group of buildings

Sculptures or virgin apartments, between the blinds

This theater, sleeping perhaps, years passed

I take the usual path, holographic spheres

Leaves roll behind me, kingdoms on the run

Then, I write a few lines, desire for freedom, season...

I look outside, out the window, at things in front of us

A subtle reason languished

The Sun, during the day, played between the branches

In its pure state, taste of a sudden rhythm...

Areas far from the resorts, little by little...

Red or coral ceilings of high transparencies

Mysterious mist, people in a hurry, dials

There was a psychedelic canvas, at the front, colorful

These joys existed, the night passed suddenly

To all our interrupted naps, to the insomnia of the holidays

Music, rue Keller, I would still raise my glass

We were waiting for the end of the incessant noises, indefinite din

Anarchic wavelength, in this time of local bazaars

The words, the word were unraveling

What can be said about the adventure?

Path, bare branches...

Near castles, with born desires

Embellished

Wandered to the edges

Meanders of forecourt

Whimsical.

5

And bouquets of flowers, I told them the colors

Purple lights on the top of towers, indistinct

As in a strange and wonderful dream

Do you remember that afternoon, unheard?

From the coast that was fleeing, in the rearview mirror...

Magical waves, Café du Progrès, the sights of aloe

This arid hour must invent the paradigm...

One night, and a sea taxi would drop me off at your house

In the west, like those ostensible trips...

We were not mismatched estates

We were this movement, words so young

In a story, and I longed for the big party

The interior space revealed itself as an art

As when the huge party still existed

On the sand, at night, knowing that summer is moving away

Without the sea, since such curves do not last...

Already, memories call me, randomly, in the distance

In a minimal way, reading books...

Always fluid, temporary distances...

Previous years, oceanic canvases

Tell anything, the thread of life...

Arid happiness, memories of trips

In the South, bare bends, on the heights

Time was like a dense slow motion

And like a multitude of images

We are more than thinking machines...

I perceived a few snippets, the country of a glance, posted ...

A thousand pages before us, through the intermittency of the heart

Like confines of imaginary spheres, attractions...

While placing them on the throne, invented...

So much desired, invisible splendor, punctuations

Blurred, festive air, meadows preserved, guarded ...

By our apogee, model, chapter, adoration

Antique shade

Impetuous

Nudity

The interlude.

6

And there was music all day, magnetizations of a smile

We stayed in the car, after observing the long and snowy park

Great ends, how many elusive moments

No effort was necessary for this empire

I clung to the first light of summer

As usual, I liked this feeling

In how many worlds, facades

Perfect harmonies, that's the time

I envied you, my senseless nights.

We superimposed clothes, eras, styles, places

To have fun, surely, to get drunk, invigorating recreations

And we remembered the happy days and the festive moments.

A time for beaches, for clubs, for libraries

That is to say, we should have been content with reality.

It was not easy to do without the imagination...

Decidedly, powerful hope was reflected...

Paragraphs, of a Creation, through it...

I turn away, now...

We need to create something

New, a Hindu or Brazilian air

Interfered, afternoon at the brûlerie.

Ah! we ran imagining other landscapes...

Maybe other lives, other parties...

On the radio, there was Francis Cabrel...

There were fields, subdivisions

You remember those delusions we had

Living in a barge on the Seine, at Bastille...

Canvases of the dawn, going to Peru, the Cordillera...

Light of Andalusia, destination Bombay...

Planetary interests, and I was thinking about this parenthesis...

From distracted anarchy, brewing, there is the clean way

Unitary, sieve of agitations, in this other space...

Temporal, without even worrying about it, art and speech...

They lingered

Beyond the walls

Titanic sculptures

From the old world.

Connections, unknown liqueurs, wanting to be everywhere

Embraced, probably stand as close as possible to enjoyment

Innocuous details reminded me of other innocuous details

Transparent night, atmosphere of the time

Golden Gate, after the debonair journey...

Feast of indescribable beauty, ecstasy

Long necklaces, going up Sainte-Catherine

In the hope of being entertained, of loving, bare back

Made up in common, I put on a t-shirt...

Then the days passed in urban alcoves

Evening was coming... And I was heading to Phillips Square...

It was snowing... It was snowing. Everything was white and quiet, fantastic

The time and the decor of the Square, of the streets, seemed frozen.

Luster of the shores, the evenings, these fantasies

As we belong only to this present

In these moments of grace, invincible journey...

To all these pages, light of centuries, sometimes

Wandering is vivid...

We cross these inscriptions

Strange sky of forces...

Parallel to dimensions.

And time passed, after a hot summer

I remembered dreams, bohemian atmosphere

On Marienplatz, from tequila to Café Pacifico

Comptoir du désert T-shirt, living a new life

Had you ever felt, ignoring the routine

This vast impression, so little palpable, of a space

Dreamlike, there was, there, an armada of projects...

Waiting for other eras, full of parallel worlds

Architectural projection, red ceilings

Or coral, high transparencies

Automatic, beyond the breathtaking view...

In her direction, drums and acidulous tones...

To the body of the brass mast

Hibiscus transi

Attached to the wave

An Icelandic diatribe.

And there was in those unlikely moments a part of mystery

Ah! summer, unparalleled, absorbed the trotteuse of the great pools

Came from other times... There were slight smiles...

It was a strange time, O flowing dials

I remembered that moment, the faces of August

Between the eyes of the trees, nomadic beaches, adventure

Yellow, walking under the sky

Purple, drizzle, excess

Squarely on the edge

Sometimes in a Deus Ex Machina Tokyo Address sweatshirt

There was simply the pleasure of walking around the city

Desire to be in the rhythm of the night, the top of the towers

From the Square, bathed in a blue halo, then purple, in the evening...

I remember all this, a world out of time

I remember that pure, detached era, boroughs

Ah! in the distance, horses of light, splendid...

Distant ecstatic, yesterday, parade of moments, this almost nothing

To I don't know what whole world...

And perfect in our eyes the essential ...

These ideas, these promises, this quest...

Of a happiness, the adventure, the perspectives.

In the past, we watched TV in the rustic living room

Wrapped in duvets, we fell asleep on the sofa...

There was a bit of Emmanuelle Béart in La Belle Noiseuse

A little bit of Garance Clavel in Everyone is looking for his cat...

Possible sequels, I knew the air soaring ...

As under the sky of rue des Taillandiers...

Creative moments, rolled up sheets, festive fatigue

Late hood of cars, tirades...

Hidden fortress

In a village...

From the Languedoc...

The years passed

Vaguely antipodes

Ancient times

Infiltrate naked and at dawn

To the overflowing vials.

9

The Square looked like an amusement park when it was bustling

And a quiet little village, when the City was removing the facilities

The Ferris wheel turned pink, then blue, white, red, and purple.

Spanish, during all these hours, enjoyments

Images escaped, runaways of a dawn

She slept naked

I undid the night, at that time

Mountain

Bushy woods.

It was the Nuit blanche

There were young people

And the not so young

Everyone was trying to exist

Beyond the stunning view, near the avenue

Sleepy, at the unstable border of the waves...

Old, appointments, whimsical festivities

Far away, the mist of the St. Lawrence was dissipating

The sea air comes to me...

Enthusiasm, virgin moment, reachable, rhythm

Fragile, of a universal regime, creates the unforgettable

Passion, as we dreamed, with plans.

There was the white night crowd

There was techno, undeniably

The Ferris wheel was mandarin...

The cottage was purple, formerly...

In the foam, in the background, and I was well...

Half a word, in speed, on Place de la Bastille...

The August temperature consumed the virginity of the evening

Vials of the troquets, these elixirs, bastions of the day before yesterday

Delights, after nights...

We accepted everything...

And this chance would mean travel

I put on a t-shirt, then a polo shirt

I saw time on my lips

Already drunk towards the River of Ink...

Tight, which no one is satisfied with

In Merovingian outfit...

There were thousands of words in the air

Freedom to live as in other times

There were garlands in the trees...

We often had half an hour in front of us...

When the kiosks had sold all their newspapers

She held a book, apart, I only went out at night

Routes, panoramas...

The future, this time

Thoughts in lettering...

I remembered that I had been someone other than myself

In another time, I remembered youth...

We had taken the road to the South, an unbeatable summer...

In my memories, there was a bit of Depeche Mode

A few steps from the dream, the world will go where it wants

We will join the nascent, bordered era

Cities, sparkling slowness, ribambelles...

Metropolises, antique respite, castles and portals

Cosmopolitan fortune...

In the streets of the great century

Inviting, under a vault...

Capital, there...

I remembered the Great Sarabande

Caresses like this with unknown borders

We couldn't do everything again, it was a long time ago

We were walking on Saint-Denis, Sainte-Catherine

When our wills have become memories

Plots of stories, I will list the passions...

Energetic, immortal, our free, earthly figures

We will have been victorious, often disobedient...

At dawn, a coffee, at night

Unrest... Ah! we were running...

Imagining other landscapes

After tubular lampshades

Perfume by shifting...

The prospects...

Let us look, naked

So unreasonable...

There were icy, distant worlds...

We no longer counted the days we fled

The processions of new data...

We had been night owls

At full speed, whispers...

Beauty has this power...

Some summer evenings, in the cellars...

Era of improvisations and mixtures

Festive, young adults of ancient times.

During the Montréal en Lumière festival

There was music, entertainment...

Unexpected colors and diffuse lighting

We joked, we talked about the future...

It was the ride, giant statues

Pinnacles of curves, so many times...

Who could have been hacienda, territory...

Eccentric, ephemeral frolics, on occasion

Always go somewhere else...

Each level unleashes its power...

Invisible, under the sheets, under the bases

Summer, at the heart of journeys, stories.

And I remembered the thread of the night

Distant beaches, relentless desire

From these hours of light and joy

No regrets, after snow parks

Sails and mirages, between hours...

And the lips, at the limit of postures ...

You were going to the foam, backwards...

It was like that, there was a happiness

Then the days passed

In urban alcoves

With the flow of time...

We had that freedom...

Euphoria...

Insouciance...

Out of bounds

Star of the night...

The order of things, time

There was Metro (it's too much)

And New York with you...

Between the giant mansions, immediate world

Walking backwards, armed with an eternal present

We will think of these few hours of happiness

From causes to consequences...

Behind translucent doors

These years, I had loved them...

In its pure state, the taste of a sudden rhythm

Driving cars in how many parties

Scattered, I ran to the domes, there were games

To wait or try to see other comings and goings

Time was another object...

Chronological, after remoteness

We were ourselves, ink...

From wanderings, we create our steps

Paper libraries...

Free drift, students...

Designers, silhouettes

Boroughs...

Getting there by road...

I recognized the atmosphere

We were listening to Talk Talk...

Or Tears for Fears...

Like the silence of centuries, these reflections...

That we love so much, when we seek...

To understand, all things invincible, initial...

They had clung to this dream, to this wandering ideal.

It all starts all over again...

So many glimmers...

Conscience...

Filled sequences

From the cosmos...

The tesserae...

We were born backwards

In the suburbs of parliaments.

On the horizon, the giants of the future

Inked pages with ease

Friends arrived by skateboard

Since the original night...

Edge of the outer moons...

At the end of the world, attraction

From the sea, thought that gives itself

To herself, for a moment

Slopes of ecstasy of this place

He's a spacer A star chaser

A spacer... He's a spacer...

One night, so many memories

Emanated from the city...

There are these scattered gems of historical

Springs the will, like an immanent force

That we no longer thought to touch, ancient splendor

After the road, slightly set back, often...

Drunk sheets, I was reading

In the rustic living room

We interfered

Between sequences...

I was rebuilding the décor...

Kitchen with bright orange walls...

A transistor swings The RTL Suitcase...

I was flipping through what was getting my hands on

Magazines, our thoughts remembered them

Overlooking the sea

We were going through foggy, intoxicating parks

We were together, apart, in the spirals

Shortly after the inauguration...

From Space, to the River of Ink...

Red ceilings of transparencies...

Mysterious mist, virtual armada

I remember the message...

Invisible pedestrians, supreme leisure

And the high lunches, raw, waltzing ...

These films of immutability...

Unfinished garden of apple pies...

There was an ocean screen on Sundays

Popular songs, the fourteenth of July

Wanderings in ochre Bermuda, so I sailed

Towards mesmerizing, almost purple horizons

She staged her departures, her returns...

The South, a feverish moment

Baz'Art Café these nights

Summer, seemed so far away...

The SCMaglev was heading towards Tokyo at five hundred km/h

In tiny translucent headphones, I listened to Bon Jovi

Some nights she had long blue hair and a tunic

Later, she could choose to be Deborah Harry's lookalike.

During my elliptical walks...

And I heard music, since the advances

Nautical, and the brass bands, the nomadic crowd...

The trip offered us the bars, and the alcove...

I exhaust this world late...

Released, have fun the turret ...

From a castle, to the bottom of a park

One entry, speeds during the summer.

Passions had fallen asleep

They had been lively and intense.

This student who was running down the street

It was me, in Bastille, in Montmartre

The pleasures were mooring...

We were taking roads...

Rise of a hundredfold possible...

The road was pristine, astonishing

Thirsty...

Satisfaction...

Invisible foundation

The clear hour...

Mergers...

Night...

In the storm...

Marine, overlooking...

15

How many wanderings had we come back from

As we had moved on...

I was listening to Big In Japan, some nights...

The truth of our eyes, on the Route des Crêtes

Escaped the roll, the asphalt stretched, infinite...

When the beginnings arranged simple places

In the air, the bastions are reborn...

The splendor would last endlessly, turns ...

Instead, we were giving America.

I preferred polo shirts to shirts

That year, old sweaters, winter

I left things to themselves...

Perspective in a half-sleep...

Yesterday, above all, brief ecstasies of a bazaar

The night was confused with vague omens...

Do you remember that incredible afternoon, the coast

Who was running away, in the rearview mirror, curves...

Feeling of adventure, hotel room...

Café, there was a high table made of light wood

I remembered that I had been another

That myself, momentum, azure hourglass...

It was not necessary to delay, course of festive forgetfulness

At the bar of alcohols in a hurry, distant stories

Everything was going to become different, and elsewhere everything was different

Desires, later, would be like immense happiness

And you dipped a hundred brushes in bowls

Colors, fine foams, period jets

We no longer counted the walked streets...

In search of nothing or maybe magic

Monarchy, buildings

The same sequence...

The idea of a wormhole...

Then belonged to the foam

In the sea of ideas

Wonders...

Dune ink

White...

16

The terraces dreamed of a better summer were taking shape

And the snow flew, covered the streets and sidewalks...

I settled into the narrative with a kind of slowness

Yesterday, with the sea...

I saw the Ridges...

A garden hardly believable

There was a large courtyard...

Inner, we would create beings

More slender, depending on the location...

Distant Silk Paths, Museum of Roads

In some youth imagined or lived...

Moving in space and time...

We knew each other like that...

One hundred years of intimate postures, like the elected

From a party, the intoxicating splendor, the drunken heroes

Under the branches of a palm tree, a banana tree

Fashion of the time, implausible music...

Leaf shovels

Ordinary patina...

The night sparkled...

Like a processor.

On the Square and in the corridors of underground Montreal...

There was the Nuit blanche crowd, there was techno

And I loved sunsets, and that purple, purple halo.

I had gone on a trip, to the size of the white paper...

The intermissions delivered me like the azure, the parades

It was necessary to hope, to compete with enthusiasm, happiness of the pages

In the sea of ideas, we loved ridges, time

Turned the eras, faces of youth, boats

Because we wanted it...

I was watering my fate...

Stolen images...

In the deckchairs of the garden

There at the heart of the century

Invisible victories

There at the agreeable cadences

Rades of spray...

17

We loved the heart of the time...

Start over endlessly, eternal revivals

As if the years had not passed

Steep descent that led to the beaches, under the pine trees

We went, panting, in the perfect heat, vegetal

Discover the subtle progressions of summer, every time

Trees are spying on me...

At the dawn of the crossings

The capitals there...

Alone in the middle of the reeds of the nature reserve...

From the pond of Pissevaches, lagoons, coots macroules

Facing the sea, I had remembered a long holiday

Secret beaches, unreasonable to Cavalière, most often

I waved my tignasse, with you, rue de la Roche...

During how many sustained walks, at the end of August...

Inside the Théâtre de Verdure, a pleasant troupe

Truce of an age of magnetism, I wanted to see behind

And I was going there in slow motion

By quiet touches

As in a thesis

Magnetic and slow...

The branches stretched to the sky

Through the window, I could see the River a little bit.

And the roads, the continual comings and goings...

Decades passed, unexpectedly...

In the distance, there was just a collective float

An absence of apprehensions, and jerks

I sometimes came back from it, with a contemplative look

It was so completely simple, a little out of the way

Millions of years

And by the clans...

Cacti, succulent

The taste of a rhythm

Pages...

Petals...

Almost a banquet

At the end of wanderings.

18

Walking on repetitive notes

I saw these acres of pure joy

Billions of emphases, brushes

From so many unreal shores, the atmosphere arose...

Cruising, below the crowded, snowy pontoons...

I was preparing an episode in a hundred parts, with its slowness

Special resource...

Arid happiness, memories...

Dimensional journeys.

We went, in the perfect heat, vegetal

Discover the subtle progressions of summer...

It was simple and at the end of a steep bend...

There were in these hours of love greatness

Winter had transcribed my meditative nights

Life is such that a sum of pages...

Shot in progressive shots, it will...

Towards the center of time, successions

Emotion, coast of utopias...

Piano of music lovers, sometimes...

On the horizon, giants of the future...

He enjoyed the moment, free suite.

I put on an Adidas sweatshirt or an Obey sweatshirt

The cadence became what it should have been

And intruded the desire for endless excitement

Unless all the impulses have been repeated

You swept the clouds, like me...

I slipped under the canvas of the idea...

New, before I wanted to restore the scheme

Fickling, picking up pine cones, ashore

Honey, licorice, money changers...

She was scrolling through the images...

Ultra-perfect versions of models

Originals, with magical sanctuaries

Hallucinogenic oils...

Tiny escapes

Intoxicate the clear waves

The insurmountable dream...

19

Planetary interests, and I was thinking about this parenthesis

In the hope of being entertained, of loving, bareback...

To all these pages, light of the centuries, sometimes...

Waiting for other eras, full of parallel worlds...

Between the eyes of the trees, nomadic beaches, adventure...

Distant ecstatic, yesterday, parade of moments, this almost nothing

I was shooting late, hood of cars, tirades...

Images escaped, runaways of a dawn

Very far away, the mist of the St. Lawrence was dissipating...

Vials of the troquets, these elixirs, bastions of the day before yesterday

Thoughts in lettering...

Metropolises, antique respite, castles and portals...

At dawn, a coffee, at night...

Era of improvisations and mixtures...

We joked, we talked about the future...

It was like that, there was a happiness...

Between the giant mansions, immediate world

I was running towards the domes, there were games

So many glimmers...

Thought that is given...

Drunk sheets, I was reading...

We were together, apart, in the spirals

Baz'Art Café of nights…

The trip offered us the bars, and the alcove...

Rise of a hundredfold possible...

When the beginnings arranged simple places

The night was confused with vague omens...

In search of nothing or maybe a magic...

There was a large courtyard...

Fashion of the time, implausible music...

The intermissions delivered me like the azure, the parades

At the dawn of the crossings...

Truce of an age of magnetism, I wanted to see behind

It was so completely simple, a little out of the way...

Arid happiness, memories...

Towards the center of time, successions...

Unless all the impulses have been repeated...